Chicken & In Love
Natalie Goldberg

Chicken & In Love

Natalie Goldberg

Cover Design by L. K. Hanson

HOLY COW! Press · MINNEAPOLIS · 1980

Grateful acknowledgement is made to the following publications in which some of these poems first appeared: *Calyx*, *Crow Call*, *Dacotah Territory*, *Identity*, *Lake Street Review*, *Milkweed Chronicle*, *Minnesota Zen Newsletter*, *Plumber's Ink*, *San Marcos Review*, and *Skyway Peninsula*.

ISBN 0-930100-04-2
Library of Congress Number: 79-90776

Cover design by L.K. Hanson
Photograph of Natalie by Lissa Halper

Second Printing, Summer 1981

Printed in the USA

Publisher's address:

HOLY COW! Press
Post Office Box 618
Minneapolis, Minnesota 55440

Member: COSMEP, COSMEP-Midwest

Other Titles from Holy Cow! Press:

Brother Songs: A Male Anthology of Poetry. Edited by Jim Perlman.
60 poems by American male poets about their fathers, sons, friends, brothers, and lovers. Graphics by Randall Scholes. 128 pages, perfect-bound, $3.50. Clothbound, $7.95

letters to tomasito, Thomas McGrath. Twenty-three poems for and about the poet's son Tomasito. 36 pages, paper, $2.00

at the barre, Candyce Clayton. Poet's first published collection.
64 pages, perfectbound, $2.50

This project is supported by a grant from the National Endowment for the Arts in Washington, D.C., a Federal agency.

For Brett

TABLE OF CONTENTS

Green Split Level

After I'd felt my first penis, 15 years old
I used to walk around the house and feel stuff
   the dishwasher hose felt most like a penis
   of anything

Mostly when I was home   green split level
I didn't think about sex much
it was a cavity in the dust sun thru window air

we moved around the house sexless
cunts tucked upward
penis behind a pant's pocket
gin in the linen closet
towels piled even
change purse in top drawer

no music   no muscles
we snuggled close at night in front of TV
and that was our warmth
like molasses

Down River

Still taste the dried white chicken meat
something's reading in my brain
long coast bus denver turnpike
asphalt all over

Why why didn't I love enough
sits in me like dried cereal
wetless veins —

Chicken shit heart!
       you coulda loved harder
       stopped all this breathless asphalt
       from fillin' you up

Empty dried up summer bean
why didn't you grab hard enough!

belched onto city streets
high heels
long earrings

Not a scent of you left —
       like old marrow
       catless gut
       all the down river

Been Here Once

chugging down coffee in a new orleans cafeteria
he wrote fast across the page across the hard tabletop
tired of each other she ate a cone wandered around
looking for something
they came to the back of a photo studio
the heat made her hot small flame burn
like a furnace in the cellar
legs opened wide   the bathroom light was on
they breathed their way home moving inside slow
clasping wet
neon signs blinked coke over slow streets

she loved out of loving through small texas towns
sleeping one night in the vinton motel
days aged her in cheap donut shops
& dreams half seen & forgotten

you can't believe emptiness can enter your own life
like a road in texas and sweep out across you

she'd been here once in this small town
so long ago cows have been eaten in the meantime
other towns she'd driven through
cattle as part of her scenery
& she in her car their sight
she'd been here once like weeds wind moan
high old telephone pole
singing on an empty night like song can't be seen
she'd been here once

No Hope

There's no help anywhere
no hope
or rest
I call a friend in Albuquerque to cry
  on his shoulder, he tells me he's lost for good
No help in the joint between my teeth
The lover man I've lived with for 3 years
  gone to Minneapolis—I could open my ancient
  war torn heart to him under heavy winter clothes

No help from anything
We hurt each other like nobody was anybody &
  the juice of our lives thirsts in the streets
No hope for any of us
  not in a glass of water, love from the sun
No hope from my false toothed mother
  my 88 year old grandmother
No swimming living hope but in our rising
  out of bed every morning
Like sea dust we move down streets early for work
Full people and all of everything in us sore
  like heartache homecake

There's no hope anywhere
nor help
nor rest
I could bleed on the streets, open my coat and cry
  there would be no help if 10,000 people listened
I could kneel to my father, crawl to him, tell him
  to grab up the years of our life together
  hold them, don't let them go, plant them, put them
  in a vase

But they're gone & I'm 30 & I'll never be yours again
  though my young heart never grew up for loving you
We'll both die, shattering our bullets hundreds of
  years apart
And Daddy we've blown it all up in photos but our lips
  will never pass over our childhoods again & still
  the rain drips, the roof leaks off the porch

And I've drained all hope like a dying rose out of love
Till not a petal of it's left & songs burst out of old
  weeping heavens

Our kidneys will fail
Our eyes move inside us
Cows'll be slaughtered for meat
Streets full of garbage
And there's no help anywhere
  under grey-skinned tired skies

Running Scared

where's all your old possibilities
& friends
& lovers
housemates
all those people
you'd goddamn starve for
cling to
make wishes all over
bury in the grass
kiss till the wind run dry

you're running down blind alleys
off city streets
gone ghost clean outta your mind
no bologna sandwich
gonna help you now,
lonely cow

Eight Nude Women On Sunday In The Mountains

Well girls
  there are some lovely titties
  out today

Ripe brown eyes
  some close to the body
   some slung by the waist

Birds are watching us
  like so much chicken feed

How come you're all gonna
  leave me today?
       huh, how come?

Listen!
  let's just decide to stay
   no one'll notice—
          really!

the air's good
your butts need exercise
there's berries to be picked
  our backs bent over
  like stones in sun

We make good meals
  Not a lot of flies
We'll write books together
     great philosophy
      poetry

I'll buy a green convertible
    we'll go tooling in the country

I don't like building
    someone else will do it
I don't like working
    someone else will earn the money

MONEY!
  We!
    We don't need money!

We have beautiful breasts
  and souls
    good sneakers
Roz has a fine hat
  and socks we've got

We have everything!

Evening Of Shambala Day

It was at a party. I started dancing with this man with
close blue eyes and whew! we danced smooth. Then I
coughed & he said you can't do that when we go on stage.
I told him I'd drink alot of tea. Then I got water in a
wine glass; he wanted to talk so I sat down. He asked what
I like? I said to eat, cook, write, sleep and to fuck. He
said that's basic. Will I see you again? I said I hope
so, at another party so we can dance. He said what about
another time. I said on the street. He said we have to
fuck on the street. If I meet a person a second time on
the street we have to fuck. I said I'll make believe I
don't know you. Then I walked 3 blocks to the car through
fog, heard my boots on sidewalk, went home another night
alone. Crawled alone into bed,
　　　　　just when I'm wanting to make love to everything—
bees, cement, trees, all women, the old man in the Boulder
Valley Administration Office, birds. Everything but soil.
Soil you can't fuck with, it's real in the hand. You hang
out with it, make things grow in it.
Lately I'm getting slower & slower. The last to finish
a meal, last down the ski slope. My roommate says I clean
slow. Soon I'll stop moving. Grow like grass in one place,
drink rain.

Boulder, Colorado

Dance With Me

When you run up against love
Watch it!
You'll never get out of it
Like bird marks on sand
it'll never leave

When you run up against love
Watch it!
Nothing'll sink as deep
or want so long
Spring so high
Never settle down
as love

It'll be like rocks in your garden
Cracks on your sidewalk
Car wheels turning
That's how fast it'll run you down!

So don't eat salt
and don't ever eat love!
Don't sit on love
or hold it like a pillow
Love will destroy
I know it

       So have some tea
       here sit with me
       the breeze outside's fine
       windows are open
       We'll dance tonight
       like curtains & arms touching

So dance with me
heave your breath in
Remember the toes!
those dots in a line
& ankle bones

Music on the street
rain in the air
rain hitting black pavement
like music
like light on ice cubes
Come and dance with me!

Spring Song

His hand
Over mine
        our liquid heat
        like sun beat
        brain cool
        barbed wire bleed

  Back a' the house
  Back a' the house
           disjoint
           disrobe
           disembark
      like a carrier pigeon
        a pale poultry
        a poplar tree

PANIC IN THE STAGE!
    she doesn't wanna blow up big as a house
        all pregnant with seed
           burst to root leaf knoll—

           shoot it out of her
           like fondling chickens
             Bigger than sky!

Opens like flower in spring
    all things
      wither and die

no reason
    no pleasin'

jus' plain nature
    flat on her back

    with all her legs open
        and all her seeds planted

So I'll Meet With You

sometime empty handed in kansas
on one single road
before green planting
you'll be hawk eye
coming toward me
we'll get some awful motel room
with orange plastic chairs
and even our love won't help the room
we'll take off our clothes
and our minds
and go to bed together
like two bears in honey

it won't matter whether your cock
stiffens or not
there won't be anything to say
when i see your body in kansas
the only moving thing on land
besides the clouds

(for rick)

Touch Cedar

Sometimes when I'm spaced—air out there, too
large for me—I go to wood. I find a piece of
cedar and saw it into stove size pieces. I
always go to my old house—the one in Talpa hill
and saw wood there.

Smell the cedar, feel its red heart, smell
its scent like clean cut potatoes. Remember
Sean Kimmey last year made me a cedar spoon.
Must of dug out the heart of a piece of cedar
and with blood on his hands carved me out a
spoon. Sugar spoon, soup spoon, apple coring
spoon.

Cedar's center flower I love most. Most I
love the twisted cedar bark. Love most the
touch, the touch of one thing in the air of
all that space. The ax touch. The split air
to clear air to reach touch cedar.

Emma

Piss slow. Yellow urine in a field. Piss. Emma used
to piss hard in the fields, like a torrent. We'd have to
leave a garbage pail twice a day at feedings full of water.
She gave more milk when she drank more.

Piss. Piss sore. Can't get my mind off the yellow piss
in Emma's stall. The smell of hay close to my nose when I'd
lift some, put it in her stall. Cow pies I'd lift up with a
pitch fork, heave 'em into the compost pile.

Loved it after it rained. Colors really came out then,
yellow straw against the dark earth. Sage smell strong as
I'd walk to Emma's. Wet soaked wood, the fence when I opened
it.

Mino would already be milking her when I'd get there.
Bent over, his head hidden in her flank, he'd be singing.
"Come on Emma, stand still." Huge animal. I was afraid of
her weight. "Steady Emma, milkings not done yet." I'd give
her more of that feed covered with molasses—it was like candy
to her.

Tits, big and hanging, pink. Mud on them from the rain.
Not soft and full like the goats. (I used to want to hold
Daisy's tit in my mouth, run my tongue along it) No. Emma's
were old cow's tits, old cow sow tits. Gave two gallons of
warm milk, when she didn't knock over the bucket with her
back hind legs.

"More of this molasses candy fer ya Emma." Felt like
I'd been there all my life, loving this cow. After milking was
done we'd lift up the wood head piece to the feeder and clear
outta the way. She'd turn three quarters round
and go into her stall. I felt like it was her dance. I'd
shut the stall door and water down the floor of the cement
feeding area; then run the water with a stiff broom down the
drain.

Wander Off Hillsides

He thinks he's gonna go
Wander off hillsides
out to midwest Minnesota country
Live in small cheap apartments
over grocery stores
Walk against red lights
Have his VW parked out
in grey cold streets

    I can't let him go
    The shape of his hips
    The warm belly I've just kissed
    All say "don't go"
    You belong with me
    Our friendship's good at meals
    Come
    I'll make you one
    Tear off some aluminum foil
    Hold your hand
    We're so familiar in bed
    I've seen your head many times
    below me on the pillow

Like a boiled bareless chicken
all my meat's naked
You can't leave this ole chicken!
She'll never get up outta bed again
Her eyes'll seek you all over streets
You've gotta be up in some tree!

This isn't our time to be over
Covers don't warm enough
Earth turns to winter
I can't eat hamburgers without you

The sky scares all birds
Still we all fly up
and out of sight
I'll follow you
Fly close to your tail
No matter!
There's no smatter of earth
can tear us apart!

Labor Day

You move further down the beach
like a stork
We cross the bridge
You never have summer shoes
Your brother complains to you
and you want to play music
Love,
      we fight over every detail
        eat plums in a park
I love you out of that tenderness of pears
rolling on a table

Your ankle bones ache
Your lips have too much will
We grow old as copper coins
Summer will never arch its neck
enough for us
Nothing will split us open
But scars there'll be
like water folding over waterfalls
We'll topple over our years
to the death of sumac by the river
Your bird feet will lift
to the step over stones

Baby,
it hurts to love in the numb sawing of time
with toes in their joints
    bending over water
and the light on the lake

Yellow Towel

Simple nights
our bare backs sleeping
and clasping what they already know
Even in the dark they did not dare
for any more   apple core

I even remember my mother, dark eyed beauty
sat in love with the womb of herself
all this lifetime in a yellow towel

Statue of dreamer, sauce of the pie,
coddled woman, she chose to be a sitter
and sat out her life

Waited for this one to end
this dull picture show, small of color
dank on too many roses
caught on too many castles
she chose to wait this one out sitting

Breathing into steamed breathing coffee
the air between them mixed a song—

sad eyed song,
eye of the cup song,
cup of the heart song,
call song,
spun song

Watchful song bought on time
Chair sitting time
long root time

After the Wedding

1

She catered our reception
when we went to New York
The food was awful
with tough pastrami
bad cookies
& greasy hor d'oeurves
She hurt
I could see it
People left their plates full
My mother said
she wanted her daughter's wedding
to be so beautiful
She thought about it later
when we drove to the beach

It hurt
because you can't take it back
you only do it once
Only have one oldest child
that marries once
for the first time
You want it to be so good
her life happy
Yes
You want all this for her

Come
new goyisha husband
Taste what I was brought up on
Taste my family
the shame we feel in loving this stuff
then thinking no one eats so good
How we know we're a bunch of aristocrats
in a world we're afraid of
Then they're really better
then we are
then we don't know
Only we cling to being Jewish
because 6,000,000 died for us

It almost doesn't matter
if there's one god who's ours
but people whose flesh burned
like lambs
and we don't know why
are not so strong
we bear up
worry
have dark eyes
deep set

We like when a non-jew comes
and we feel comfortable
Yes
we like that fine
So maybe we're not so bad
though we look down alot
the old are bent
mostly die aging with wrinkles
and the bone bent of their nose

We seem to die a different death
under a different sky
with old hanging breasts
and hearts breaking

Don't put up a headstone till a year later
Then the whole family
goes out there again
in autumn bare branches
Watches the final stone put over their head
now we know it's really real
they're really dead

There isn't much consolation in god
after all our bellowing about religion
They're just really dead
in the dirt
We go home
eat for seven days
look across the dining room table
to each other

The little ones wear nice dresses
You want them around
give them cookies
This is the new skin
Here *mon tatala*
have a little something
Grandpa would have liked it
Ahh, my *chena*
one god should only help us

Chicken Lesson

I'm decked out on the couch
trying to find a poem
in my squirrelly notebook
when he comes home
I don't look up
Hope he has flowers for me—
I've waited these hours
for chicken
roasting in a pan
Fat melting
mixing with the paprika
I rubbed in the skin hours ago

"You do it like this"
with wedding ring on left hand
you rub the chicken
Open its wings
Pull out some of the fat
between skin and meat
Too much'll make you sick
Sit on the couch while it cooks
The heat rises in it
Up to tender breast
the tenderest
and the tougher thighs

It drips clear when it's done
The red blood rises in cooking
and boils into gravy
It drips clear when it's done
Don't ever stuff it
Leave it gaping like some lidless jar
Eat chicken meat like it's your meat
None of it can go to waste

Watch closely how your husband eats
What part he wants—
    the brown thigh
    he must have cloudy eyes
    his desire is weak
    but he loves you good
He doesn't reach for skin
One helping's enough—
    he'll have light dreams tonight
    wake at 2 a.m.
    then fall back to sleep again

Work-A-Day

My husband rocks across from me
We're married
& still I'm lonely
Not because of him
but because loneliness
is the one empty thing we walk through
like grass and trees

We leave for work
as the sun hits the horizon
The car is cold
We travel our separate ways all day

He crosses the street
climbs stairs
looks at his reflection in windows
eats lunch
jingles change in his pockets

I move in Central High School halls
with people—I know all people
are people—
They feel so different
so little to touch ground on
One eats a brown sugar donut
sips coke
Another just spent 4 days
at a Las Vegas convention—

We come to each other I'm so thirsty for him
for soft human touch
Instead we argue about the bed not made
crumbs on the table
Can't come to touch him
because this is too human in a brittle day

My always friend & our faraway desires
our home together
where we place our sweaters
rolled paired socks
his white underwear
the shoes beside the door
Where the plants breathe with us
all night long
Loneliness wraps itself
around our apartment on 8th street
across from mr. steak
the mobil gas station
Where the heaters keep working
& plugs stay in sockets all night long

Two Iowa Farmers

We know each other too long
Make love like two Iowa farmers
in plaid flannel nightgowns—
He gets on top
licks a flame in her
then can't keep it up
His big thing
withered to a worm in rain

She's large under warm covers
Half wanting it
Half wanting sleep
in a mouth that doesn't bother
with lipstick
He reaches down
like it was molasses puddin'
Moves her mound of dry hay
She rocks her eyes back
dreams of berries
goose down
tar poured in the feeding station
She winds up heaving like windmills
Station wagon come to a stop
He pulls out the key
She's done for
but has some duty still
in her blind body

He mounts
this time for himself

for his rows of sweet corn
the tractor
for the old wood barn
He's movin' with it all
It's hard through thick mud
His heart's pounding
   huge flights of birds
   lift their autumn wings
He arches his neck like a dog's
full moon night
Then takes a nose dive like a paper plane
It's all over
What he was doin' anyhow
Finds this warm body
like thick cream
snorin' under him
He wonders:
Only Iowa!
could make it this good

Farm Wife

You gotta coupla ugly kids
a dry dirt farm
where the wind covers anything
if there ever was beauty out there
I don't care to look these days
If the stew gets stale
I just add more salt
It's good enough for that filly
that sweet thing
Pretty coat of skin
Good and sleek short hair

My husband
if I can remember back that far
had some sleekness in him
in his butt
The little cherry thing
would roll over me like a music band
We'd play a fat back polka then
My tongue like a pink ham
would hang out my young teeth
Nothing but squirrel stew
in those days
A lot of broken fences
Sweat down his back
I'd try to frisk up my lashes
with maybelline brown

My husband
he'd like to play on my small fears
Carry a garter snake he found
back of the ditch
Bring it in the house
I'd start screaming
He'd toss it out the front door
wrestle me to the couch
Later on
his coming in me was like sawdust
ripped out of a flour bag

All the bisquits & gravy
I got good at baking
made us two big cows
Remember staring at 'em
feeding on grass and dandylions
when I was thinner than a nylon slip
Afraid they'd step on me
Now I'm one of 'em
Old cow looks out
at those colored fall leaves

My son
he marry some girl in the south county
We never see 'em
One of their brats
broke granny's sugar jar
One pee'd once laying on our couch
Still got the stain
No smell anymore though
Bad as when the yellow tomcat
got big and flustered
when a female was around
Had to spray himself all over the place
like a ferris wheel

We eat quail once in a while
That's good
But it doesn't count for much
in the afternoon
when you know all you got ahead
is night time
I can't read much for anything
Looked through the catalogue
enough times now
I know what's gonna be on the next page
So I've taken to mending stockings
They're not warm enough in winter
Too hot in summer
But a body's got time
You got to do something with it
So it don't catch you short
Bite you in the butt

Beggars Against Winter

This is good
to love some human being in a life
reach across the table as they lift coffee to mouth
to know the hand that curls around the cup

This one time in more important things
love one human being besides yourself
hold thick lips to his
see the face of his eyes even when the lights are out
the dim lashes of sleep against his pillow
sleep like beggars against winter

Every storm breaks your back for the last time
you walk more bent
Smoke curls from a cigarette in a restaurant
This you'll love—
even the cold nights
the faceless menu
the uneven talk
Snow of last November
will still be there like bread crust
the ice
the solid black asphalt
cold car
keys in hand
frost will already be forming on the windshield

This you'll love & more—
the way he turns to you in a night
with the starless ceiling above you
the bone of his knee back curve tired head
on the pillow
How does he sleep?

All night next to you fitlessly & has no need to talk
knows the body next to his like warmed egg
knows the stars in some evenings
shine through blizzards

Every night is a blizzard in the blind eyes of lovers
like dwarfs we fall asleep under snow that fills us
all our lives
This is good the winter here
It tells you your bones are not forever
but crack like evening sky
into more light
You are not forever
And if I was separated from him in a blizzard
with school children
I would love them like myself
and he would love
who he is with

Rolling Mouth
at the 25th street laundromat

Isn't it our juice together
makes sun on table

Isn't it our juice together
you me and sun
make apples turn in heat

You me sun apple
make porcelain sinks cold
in morning touch

Isn't it you me sun apple sink
make clean wash
in rolling mouth machines

Isn't it you me
sun apple sink machine
make song make skip
make whistle & hum

Isn't it you me carwash cattle
tail wag pollywog!
make the streets rain
full of mud
Isn't it mud makes love
Isn't it dry weeds make autumn
make ice
make cold

Isn't it you me pollywog and cattle
make dish
big porcelain dish
with sink to wash face
big toe

You me bend over water
Isn't it you me
cup hand
drink water

Apple sun
come along
follow up

Granny Rose

Said good-by to granny Rose last night
She already in bed; 7:10 in evening I show up,
heaters hot, she half sleeping in white slip,
says it's her nightgown. Soft bones under
her skin, white, still smooth hanging,
deep set eyes, hook nose, face shrunken,
still looking sensuous old
withered mother.

She's happy to see us (Romi came too).
She thinking it was another day over,
we bring her soft ice cream in plastic cup.
She puts on peach sweater over slip
and sits in chair next to bed. Very lucid
this time of day: remembers last week
she came home for three days. We ate
turkey, saw family movies, she sang songs
from *Oklahoma*. Pictures of her grandchildren,
great grandchildren on bureau, all framed.

Her roommate, 92, watches television
over by next bed. Wears flower cotton
dress robe. I go over to say hello.
"Tell your grandmother to wear a nightgown
to bed" I want to say my grandmother's
a hippy, don't though. Print velvet
wallpaper, two plants on windowsill
I figure my grandmother forgets to water,
sure the nurse keeps them alive.

Romi too eats some of the ice cream.
My grandmother's not wearing glasses now,
the skin around her eyes dark,
she tells us she hopes we get married.
Me first, I'm the oldest, then I'll fix
Romi up—the way Dora did to her.

She still looks sort of supple luscious
leaning back in her chair, white short hair,
88 years old.
Thinks we're very grown up to drive there
at night alone. I keep kissing her neck,
she laughs. I'm filled with longing
not to leave her.

Romi sitting hunched over, next to me on the bed.
It's so early night, she gets up to kiss us good-by.
I see her thin shriveled face, thin lips
shaped into a pucker, she leans over to kiss Romi,
their lips meet. And now me, the same.
I feel a little of her spittle.
We go out fast, past her roommate.

Dream

I smell my grandmother
I'm standing over her
smelling her smell
Taking it in forever
It's a good smell
no one will smell like it again

She has a thick pencil
sticking out the collar of her blouse
She's sitting in a wheel chair
It's getting near the end
I'm not going to wake up
because I want to stay with her smell
her warm small head
This is the last time
so any moment counts
Once she'll be dead
she'll be dead for a long time

She's had an operation
Instead of taking the elevator
she took the exit
fell down a long flight of stairs
Then she wanted to get out
of the wheel chair
fell
and got stitches on her forehead

I'm taking in this smell
for the last time
that smell
that warm smell
that warm blue smell

Slow Seeing the World Go Round

She drinks water
she does
she drinks water

She my grandma
  drinks water till
    there's no more water

She tells her story
she has a good story
she marries her grandpa
they meet in brooklyn
go riding on horse & buggy
it rain all over streets
the sky is good sky
they rain in their hearts
and family come down
they own chicken market
all eggs are good eggs

She walks across brooklyn bridge
sell candies
model hat
she good and never did bad
she drank water till water all gone
she good in the heart of her mouth
she back far in her head
she rain children
one black eyed mother of me
  She I love She I love
    She I love

It rain all their life
till it stop raining
till sky went away
eyes went away
horse & buggy flew
all all cobbled streets
went far away

She goes
She goes
 Don't go
She still goes
 Don't go
She goes
 Her sister gone
 No more food
She goes
 No more black shoes
 plastic bag
 prune
 salt
She goes

She never played the piano
she won't sing
she go with her feet
she going all the way
like a kite in the sky

Orange Bowl

Grandpa had an orange bowl that I never no-
ticed. Sure. Of course I noticed it; I
knew it was grandpa's but I never saw it, the
way you never see things that are there every-
day speaking to you but you never notice
them except to water them or put them away or
clean them. So then afterwards you try so
hard to remember them, to let them comfort you
and remind you about the nice life you had.
Yeah. And I guess it was nice when grandpa
was around. He taught me stuff like cleaning
the crumbs off the table and always wearing
shoes so I wouldn't step on needles and to
soak all the silverware in the dirty pot when
I washed dishes to save soap. I was short then
and the screen windows were always open because
it was summer and there was that summer smell
that never really smelled but you seemed to
take it in through your nose anyway.

And among the things I washed and dripped with
water was this shiny orange bowl the color of
a Florida orange after its been dyed orange.
I feel it now wet and clean, surrounded by the
air that was summer. He ate cornflakes in it
every morning and the flakes got soggy and stuck
to the sides of the bowl and sometimes I would
pick them with my fingers and eat them. It
was fun being short, because then grandpa could
put his arm around my waist when I stood and he
sat and ate his cornflakes. That isn't really
the reason it was fun being short; there is no
real reason. It was just good to be there that
summer with the screened windows and the orange
bowl and be short and hungry and have cornflakes.

I don't know. Maybe grandpa didn't even matter.
He died anyway. He just helped to set the scene.
You know, having an orange bowl and being taller
so I knew I was shorter and marrying grandma so
eventually I could wash dishes with him sometime
in my life and remember it some other time in my
life. It was fun though I didn't know it then,
in the same way I never really saw the orange
bowl. Instead I was listening to the bells of
the Good Humor man and scratching mosquitoes on
my legs with the heel of my sneaker while I stood
by the sink.

You might think I washed dishes a lot when I was
young. I didn't. Grandpa didn't like the way I
did them. But somehow, I'm remembering this one
time when I did and when I was short and when
Grandpa was alive.

To Grandpa, deceased and to R.S. alive

The many faces of the clock
Have whiskers that won't stay put
Schools, offices, factories
Are ruled by rebellious, gyrating moustaches

And so
Do not think about time
Your heart knows its duration
When the last red raspberry is eaten
And the Jewish newspaper is no longer important
And you love your grandchildren with the rhythm of existence

your heart will stop

Upon sending the above poem to my parents. . . . . .

Mother: You're poem was fantastic. When did you find out
you had such talent? Did it just come upon you?

——: Nooooo. . . . . . I just didn't have much confidence.

Mother: Oh, but now you do. Well, you're quite a gal. Daddy
didn't understand the first part about whiskers but I explained
it to him. The whiskers are the hands of the clock. Right?

——: . . . yes . . .

Mother: Now, what's R.S.?

——: That's Rob—he wrote me a letter asking what I thought
about time and I wrote this.

Mother: Oh . . .Well that was very inappropriate to write
to him when it was a poem to grandma and grandpa.

——: What! It isn't to grandma! I didn't sit down
and decide to write a poem to even grandpa but as I thought
about death, the only experience I've had of it was with him.

Mother: oh yes, yes, I see . . . Well! We loved your poem.
We're going to have it read at the unveiling next week.
Here's your father.

    Nat,
        I loved your poem. It made me cry.
    Except that bad part.

——: You mean "your heart will stop"

    Ohhhhh. . .
        don't say it. It made me think of my own life.

    But then we have no raspberries in the house.
    I like strawberries better anyway. What's R.S.?

——: It's also to Rob.

    There's no "S" in Rob.

——: Daddy, it's his initials. He wrote me about time.

    Time!
        What a peculiar thing to write about . . .
        I only think about who's winning in the sixth race.
        yes, well, there's alot of songs written about time
                    I guess . . .

Just in time . . . I met you just in time.

or

 As time goes by . .

or

 Time is a many splendored thing

No, that was about love . . . yes, love . . .
Nat,
    Write some poems to me, will ya?

Be Tree

let ice bend you
lend you
sun warm you
wind crack you
be in air elegant
turn with the land
be tree

standing through years
chipmunks gulls
torn open by fox
lichen crawl over rocks

be tree!
be mover in space
be silent grower
be all of me
against lake cold winter

beside barn
near road
close to porch
be bent
be strong
sing wind
sink deep
be tree

One More Word

When the eyes go
When the ears go
When the nose goes

    lemme keep my tongue
    lemme keep my teeth

When the skin goes
When the feet go
When the bones go

    lemme keep my tongue
    lemme keep my tongue!

    that flapper
    that talker
    that ole time taster

The bones may know
The eyes may see
The ears may hear

But it's the tongue that talks

    eyeless & skinless
    homeless & hopeless

Let the tongue be!
    that drooler
    that licker
    that ole time lover

Born and raised in New York, Natalie has lived most recently in Taos, New Mexico and Boulder, Colorado, before making her home two years ago in Minneapolis. She has taught writing workshops at the University of New Mexico, Minneapolis Art Institute, Lama Foundation and Northeast College in Norfolk, Nebraska as well as to nuns, high school dropouts, hippie kids and women in Taos and old people in Saint Paul, Minnesota. At Naropa Institute, she studied poetry with Allen Ginsberg. This is her first book of poems.